A Game of Marbles

By

Sue Blood Haynes, Ph.D.

Illustrated by:

Peggy Blood, Ph.D.

This book is a work of fiction. Places, events, and situations in this story are purely fictional. Any resemblance to actual persons, living or dead, is coincidental.

ISBN: 1-4033-2573-1 (e-book)
ISBN: 1-4033-2574-X (Paperback)
ISBN: 1-4033-2575-8 (Hardcover)

Library of Congress Control Number: 2002091588

This book is printed on acid free paper.

Printed in the United States of America
Bloomington, IN

1stBooks - rev. 12/01/03

Contents

iv

CHAPTER 1
MY FRIENDS

It was fun living on 11th street.

All my best friends lived on this street, including my dog Spike.

Spike was a light brown German shepherd dog. He would guard the house when no one was home.

Spike would bark only at uninvited guest when no one was home. Once a strange foot stepped into the yard, he would bark fiercely and turn flips to scare them away.

Spike would never bite anyone. He was a good guard dog.

Spike had his head set like a clock to wake me up every morning for school.

Bowwow! Bowwow! Goes Spike, scratching on my window.

His barks woke me up, but I would turn over in the bed, pull the covers over my head, and go back to sleep.

My mom, Tracy, would come into the room and chant, "Get up Charles! Get up now!"

I did not move a muscle.

My mom would then pull off the covers and chant again, "GET UP! GET UP!"

The air was cold. My body was shaking. I jumped straight up out of the bed.

I grabbed my pants, shirt, and shoes and put them on quickly.

Still shaking I ran to the bathroom.

The door was locked.

My two sisters were in the bathroom. They would always hold the bathroom up in the mornings for long periods of time.

I knocked on the bathroom door and said, "Hurry up! Please come out of the bathroom. I need to use it."

My sisters yelled through the door, "Sorry we are not finish, sleepy head."

I called out to my mom, "Mom tell Nora and Elsie to come out the bathroom. I need to use it."

Mom called out to my sisters, "Nora and Elsie come out the bathroom? Right now!" She said.

"OK mom!" They said. My sister's then unlocked the door and came out of the bathroom.

I went into the bathroom and turned the water on in the bathtub. As the water fell into the tub I went splash! splash! With only my hands into the tub, I pretended as if I was taking a bath as my hands swirled quickly in the water. Then with a big swish! I swirled the water again in a circular motion as if I was taking a bath. I then let the water out, brushed my teeth and washed my face.

"Are you finished washing up Charles?" My mom asked.

"Yes mom," I said unlocking the door and coming out to go back into my bedroom to make my bed. While in my bedroom, I heard my mom call out to me.

"Come eat your breakfast Charles. Come now!" she said. "So you won't be late for school."

My dad always got up very early to go to work. Sometimes he would cook breakfast.

I loved it when he would cook stewed tomatoes.

"What's for breakfast mom?" I asked.

"Hot oatmeal," she replied.

"Oh no," I said to myself. "I hate oatmeal. Why didn't dad cook breakfast?"

I forced the oatmeal down while my mom watched me eat.

"Eat all the oatmeal in your bowl," she said, "and let me see you swallow it."

Mom would watch me eat, because sometimes, I would stuff all the oatmeal in my mouth.

My jaws would be puffed out, and when I got outside I would spit it out.

"Get your books and lunch Charles," Mom said, "and hurry to school."

"What's in my lunch, Mom?" I asked. She replied, "Peanut Butter and jelly."

This was my favorite lunch.

I had a long walk to school. I never walked alone. I walked to school with my friends Percy and Daniel. It took us 20 minutes to walk to school. Our school was about a mile from our home.

I got my books and lunch sack and ran next door to Percy's house.

"Percy!" I called out. "Lets go!"

Percy yelled through the door, "OK! I am coming, Charles."

Percy's father did not live with them. He had two older sisters.

His mom, Sarah, worked all day ironing clothes for money to support the family.

Sometimes there were no clothes to iron and she did not make any money.

Percy sometimes had no breakfast.

Percy ran out the house with his books. He did not have a lunch and he did not have on any shoes.

"Did you forget your lunch, Percy?" I asked.

"No," said Percy. "I have no lunch."

"You can share my lunch, Percy," I said.

"Thank you, Charles," said Percy. "Maybe the teacher will bring some treats too."

Percy also had no school shoes. He went to school barefoot everyday.

The only shoes he had were a pair of sandals.

His sandals were Sunday shoes, which he wore to church. When the straps broke on his sandals he would pin them on with a safety pin or tie them on with a string.

Percy and I went next door to Daniel's home.

"Daniel!" We called out. "Lets go!"

Daniel yelled back, "OK! I am coming."

Daniel had six sisters and brothers. He was the youngest son.

His dad worked across the street from their home in their barbershop. Daniel's father would tell all his customers, "I helped to make Madame C.J. Walker the first Negro woman millionaire. I use all of her hair products to wash and process customer's hair." On Saturday the William's worked all day and most of the night styling people's hair. All the men in the neighborhood came to get their hair styled at their barbershop.

Mrs. William's always complained to Daniel for getting holes in the sole of his tennis shoes. The sole of the tennis shoes were thin rubber when new. Playing one game of basketball on the asphalt court would be all the tennis shoe could stand. After the game we all would be walking on the ground. Top of the shoe new and the bottom, oh well history, from playing basketball at school.

"Daniel I need you to cut some cardboard soles for my tennis," I said. Daniel was good at cutting cardboard the perfect shoe size.

"OK, Charles put your shoe on top of this stiff cardboard." Daniel got the cardboard from his dad's barbershop. After Daniel cut the cardboard I put it into my tennis to cover the holes. The cardboard would protect our feet from walking on the ground.

Daniel's lunch would always be made with biscuits. Sometimes the biscuit would have jelly between it, and sometimes the biscuit would have molasses between it.

"Daniel did you eat breakfast?" asked Percy.

"Yes," said Daniel, "I had hot biscuits, fatback and molasses for breakfast."

"Then why are you eating your lunch?"

"Because the children at school will poke fun at me having a biscuit for lunch."

Daniel felt so bad when children would poke fun at him.

Percy and I never poked fun at him or anyone else. Daniel continued to explain to Percy and I, "If I eat the biscuit before I get to school my stomach will be full and I will not need any lunch."

"No biscuit, no shame, no hurt," said Daniel. Sometimes he would throw his lunch away before he got to school.

We started running to school so we could play before the bell rang for class.

CHAPTER 2
SCHOOL

There were three separate schools in my hometown. The Mexican and Chinese children attended school together. White children attended a separate school.

We attended the school for Negroes. Our school was just over the railroad tracks.

The school was a wood building that had four classrooms. Eight grades were taught at the school. Two grades were taught in each classroom. The classrooms were jammed full of desk. Some desks were in the hallway.

Children sitting in the hallway would trade seats inside the classroom when the teacher would teach the opposite grade.

As Daniel, Percy and I entered the school playground before class, some of our classmates were shooting hoops.

"Let's join in on the game of basketball," I said. "I can't today," said Daniel. "My shoes have holes from playing basketball yesterday and my feet are sore."

"I can't shoot hoops today either," said Percy. The asphalt was rough on my feet yesterday also. I fell and got wholes in the knees of my new pants."

"Lets play some touch football," said Percy.

"Yeah," said Daniel, "hurry and get the football before the bell rings."

We played touch football until the bell rang for class.

When the bell rang, we got in line to march into the classroom. We would line up according to our seat in the classroom. Percy was tall so he sat in the back row. He was always first in line. Daniel sat in the middle of the room and I sat in the hallway.

Our principle, Mr. Sawyer, would come out and greet all the children before we went into the classroom. He would say, "I want all you children to do good work today and to obey your teacher. I don't want to see any of you in my office today. OK?" All the children would say, "Yes Mr. Sawyer."

Mr. Sawyer and all the teachers lived in our neighborhood. They knew all our parents.

If we act up in the classroom or on the playground, we would have to face Mr. Sawyer and the ruler. POW! He hit right in the palm of our hand.

The teacher had our classroom divided into two sections. The fifth grade sat to the right of the room and the six grade sat to the left of the room.

When the fifth grade had math class the six grade had a study period.

We had no library at school but our teacher set up a library system in the classroom. We could check out the books that our teacher had gathered from used bookstores and her friends.

The books we were taught from were used books, also. When the white schools would get new books we got their old books.

Our teacher, Mrs. Banks, would put a marking in each book. The marking would state the condition of the book.

11

The book was marked either, 'Good' 'Fair' or 'Poor'. At the end of the year we had to return the books in the same condition so the next class could use them.

My reading book marked "Fair" had torn pages.

The math book marked "Fair" had worn pages and some missing pages.

Mrs. Banks did not allow the children to complain about the used books. She always said, "A library book is a used book. All books are made to be used. If a page is missing, you will copy it from my book. Never mind these used books. You will learn and you will become the best."

In reading class, Mrs. Banks always called on us to stand and read a page out loud.

"Percy," she said, "stand and read page 6."

Percy never missed a word.

"Now Daniel stand and read page 7."

Daniel would always miss a word.

If we missed a word, she would say, "What is the word child? Spell it. Now sound it out by syllables."

If they still missed it, she would say, "What is the word class?" The class would all say the word out loud.

"Now child, say the word 5 times, now write it 100 times, and turn it into me. No recess until you finish." "WOW!" Said Daniel. Mrs. Banks was hard, but we learned.

"Any questions on this reading assignment?" Mrs. Banks asked.

I put my hand up, "Yes Charles," she said.

"In our reading assignment why are some people called Colored and some called Negroes?"

Mrs. Banks hesitated for a moment looking at the pages in the reader, and then she said, "There are no differences in the words. Just some conflicting views on the term Colored and Negro."

"Does anyone know why?" She asked.

"Would anyone like to explain?" She asked again. No one put his or her hand up to answer.

"Well it goes back to your roots," she explained.

"Charles, I knew your grandfather, he was French. Your grandmother was African. You are the product of two roots. However, no one can define your roots but your ancestors," Mrs. Banks explained.

"Who are my ancestors Mrs. Banks?" I asked.

"Charles," she said, "they are people for which your grandparents must identify within their family roots."

"But Mrs. Banks," I said, "I am still confused, where did the word colored people come from?" "Charles," she said, "white nor black is a color. The mixture of the two makes color, Colored People.

Some of the authors call us colored people because they think it sounds more acceptable to us. The word Negro sometimes is mispronounced sounding negative," she explained.

"Anymore questions?" She asked. No one put his or her hand up. "You were a good class today. Class dismissed." Percy put his hand up. "Yes Percy," she said. "Mrs. Banks since we were good, does this mean you will bring us a treat tomorrow?"

"I don't know," said the teacher, "I will decide later."

We loved our teacher and she loved for us to learn.

All the children in the neighborhood went to school. The school would check on children if they did not show up for school. There were no school dropouts.

On sunny days we ate our lunch outside and played on the playground.

The playground at school was all dirt. When it rained it became muddy. We all played in the mud at school and at home. Some of us got good at it making mud cakes and mud figurines.

On rainy and cold days we ate our lunches in the classroom and played games inside.

Sometimes our teacher would bring treats to school to reward us for doing good work in school.

The treats were sometimes Rice Crispy squares made with marshmallows. And sometimes the treats would be sandwiches.

Sometimes, these treats would be the only food some children had to eat for lunch. If they were hungry, they had to wait until they went home. There was no cafeteria where they could get lunch.

CHAPTER 3
THE WALK HOME

After school we had so much fun walking on the dusty roads home.

"Get that can Percy! Lets see who can kick it the farthest," said Daniel.

"No way", said Percy, "I am not going in those sticker bushes barefoot to get a can."

"I'll get the can out the berry vines and I will kick it first." "OK Charles get the can and watch out for a snake," Said Daniel.

We continued kicking the can up the street towards home.

From the porch of Mrs. Bee's home, we heard a soft voice say, "Hello boys, how was school today?"

"Hi! Mrs. Bee," we replied.

"School was good."

"Tell your parents hello for me." she said.

"Yes, madam."

"I like Mrs. Bee," said Percy. "She gives my mom clothes for us. She gets the clothes from her work.

She cleans homes for rich white people."

"Yes, I like her too," said Daniel. "One day I forgot to speak to her and she told my mom, I guess you know what came next."

"I know," said Percy, "You had to get a switch from that Weeping Willow tree in your yard and your mom whipped you."

My mom says, "Daniel, go get me two thin limbs from the Weeping Willow tree. She twists the thin limbs together to make a switch. She then lean back and those limbs swish and whistle in the air as she comes down with them across my butt. Now that really hurts."

17

"Yeah, when my mom whips me, I run all over the house. She runs behind me hitting me with the switch. I scream out loud! Please stop mom? I won't do it again!" She says, "I know you won't Charles."

My mom keeps running after me until I slide under the bed.

Our beds are iron and on rollers.

She rolls the bed back and forth, trying to get me from under the bed. But I hold on to the slats and I slide with the bed.

My mom gets so tired until she says, "OK! You stay under there. You will have to come out and when you do, you will get it again Charles."

"Believe me, my mom has a long memory. She never forgets."

"My mom always whips me when my dad is gone. My dad never whips me. He will talk to me and when he finishes, I know he meant it. I never do that again."

"Get out of the street!" Percy yelled out.

"Here comes a car."

The car was traveling fast and a trail of dust was behind the car.

We fanned the dust with our hands. The dust was everywhere.

It got into our face, on our clothes and skin.

Spike would always run to meet us after school.

There was so much dust that we did not see Spike running to meet us.

Spike broke through the dust barking, "Bowwow! Bowwow!" He jumped up on me.

I was so glad to see him. I rubbed him on his head and hugged him saying, "Hi Spike, you are a good dog." Spike would waggle his tail in approval. Daniel and Percy also patted Spike on his back and said, "Good dog Spike!"

We enjoyed playing with Spike. We would take turns throwing a stick as far as we could. Spike would run and get the stick and bring it back.

We had fun running and playing with Spike until we reached home.

CHAPTER 4
A DIVIDED CITY

The railroad tracks divided neighborhoods.

The Mexicans, Chinese and Colored people lived together on one side of the railroad tracks and white people lived on the other side of the railroad tracks.

The railroad tracks were the invisible wall dividing a town named the same but visible different.

Percy's mom would take us with her some days, as she gathered clothes to be washed and ironed from people who lived on the other side of the railroad tracks.

We loved to walk on the paved sidewalks. When cars would go by there was no dust because the streets were paved.

"Mrs. Julin," I said, "the sun shines different in the white neighborhood."

Mrs. Julin replied, "No Charles, the sun shines the same everywhere. The air is just fresher over here."

Most of the homes Mrs. Julin gathered clothes from were just small brick homes, but today she stopped at a huge brick and stone house.

"Mom!" Percy said, "This house is like a mansion! WOW! We have never stopped here before. Can we come into the house with you?"

Mrs. Julin would let the boys come into some of the homes with her if the maid was there.

Mrs. Julin knocked on the back door. The maid came to the door. "Can I help you," she said.

"I am Mrs. Julin. I came for the laundry."

"I am Mrs. Cooper, the house maid. I am gathering the laundry now," the maid responded. "Come in the house where it is cool while I get the laundry for you. Are these your sons?"

"This is my son Percy, the other boys are Charles and Daniel. They live in my neighborhood," answered Mrs. Julin.

Most of the homes in this neighborhood were on a whole block of land and the houses looked as if they were half a block in size.

Mrs. Julin and the boys came into the house.

Daniel said, "Mrs. Cooper, can you show us around in this house."

Mrs. Cooper responded, "Sure come with me."

She began to tell us about the house. "This house is an antebellum house," the maid said. "Do you boys know what is meant by an antebellum house." "No madam," the boys responded. "This house was built before the Civil War and it survived the war. This house is classified as a mansion. The forum we are standing in is large enough to entertain 300 guests. This house has 8 bedrooms, four separate sitting areas, a library, a office room, game room and 9 bathrooms," she said. "We are going upstairs to the bedrooms and sitting areas."

We all went up this circular stairwell that was hardwood. The hardwood was shining like glass with a streamer of red carpet in the center. The stairwell seemed as wide as our street. We entered a large hallway that had lots of doors. The maid opened double doors to a large room.

"This is the master bedroom," the maid said.

"WOW!" said Daniel. "This bedroom is as big as our whole house!" The maid continued showing Mrs. Julin and the boys the house. "This master bedroom has a fireplace sitting room, study room, and a 'His' and 'Her' bathroom with a walk-in closet off each bathroom. All the floors in this house are Swedish finished white oak hardwood."

"This house is so big it's spooky!" I said.

"Yeah!" said Percy, "we could play hide-and-go-seek in this house and no one would find us.

"Yeah!" I said, "my mom would never catch me in this house to whip me. I would tire her out just running from room to room!"

Daniel looked out from the upstairs balcony and said, "Look Charles and Percy at the beautiful birds chirping.

They are all different colors. They have a bird house up in the tree."

The maid finished bundling the clothes for Mrs. Julin to take home to launder. We left this mansion to return home.

On the walk home we came upon a school. It was a large brick building with an upstairs and a downstairs. The playground was paved with flowers and shrubs. The basketball rims had nets. The football field had green grass with concrete covered bleachers.

"Mrs. Julin, what school is this?" asked Daniel.

"This is the school for white children, Daniel. When I attended school, I would come here with the teacher to pick up the old used books for our school. They have lots of classrooms and a library full of all kind of books."

"We don't have a library at our school. Sometimes our teacher takes us on field trips and she points out the public library. Our teacher says Negro People are not allowed to go into the Public library. One day she hopes we will be able to use the library."

We crossed the railroad track and soon reached home.

CHAPTER 5
RIDING ON THE TRAIN

The train going through the neighborhood was a source of entertainment. We use to go down to the railroad tracks and wave at the people on the train as the train zoomed by. The Negro people on the train would be so glad to see us. They would smile and wave back. We would be so happy when someone would get off the train to visit us.

The people would get off the train with their clothes in trunks and boxes. Everyone would be carrying a shoebox. The shoebox was a most needed and very important box in our neighborhood.

The shoebox was used for a lunch box. People would tie a string around the shoebox for a handle so it could be carried easily.

Negro people could not eat in the dining car on the train. Most of them could not afford to order food from the diner either. So when they got hungry out came the shoebox.

In the shoebox would be fried chicken, pound cake, biscuits, peanut butter and jelly.

Negro people would also travel with large boxes, tied up with rope. Some of them could not afford a trunk for travel. The boxes would be their trunks. The boxes would be so heavy. Sometimes four people would have to carry them. My grandma would also bring a hatbox full of hats for Church. She loved to dress up for church.

We had to travel along the side of a dirt and gravel road to get home. The cars would fly by leaving a cloud of dust. The dust would cloud our vision. All the children in the neighborhood would help to get the boxes home. We would struggle with the boxes down the dirt-trailed narrow sidewalk created by foot traffic. Finally we would reach home and everyone would hug and kiss.

CHAPTER 6
LIVING CONDITIONS

Most of the Negro people lived in the same neighborhood in cities and towns. The neighborhood often was a source of income and an economic base for Negro people.

My dad often talked economic, social and political issues after dinner as we sat around the table. His favorite topic was capitalism and how it worked in the Negro community.

Today's dinner was no special occasion but mom had made some of our special dessert, bread pudding with lemon sauce. As we enjoyed the pudding dad said, "Charles I want you to always remember how I was able to provide for this family. Our community has a lot to do with our economic base. The dollar turns over 20 times in our community."

"Dad how does the dollar turn over 20 times?" I asked.

"Well, lets see," said Dad. "This nice home you live in was architect by Mr. Robertson. Deacon Lee did the plumbing.

The electrical was by Mr. Amos. Mr. Lyle down the street is an expert at building concrete foundations. Do you remember Mr. Anderson? He passed away about three years ago. He was the best brick mason in town. He help build most of the buildings down town and he helped me build our home."

"Dad, did Mr. Ryles make our cabinets?"

"Yes son, and old man Roberts at the age of 65 put the roof on.

Johnny learned carpentry while helping to build our home. He is a fine carpenter today.

You see Son, the dollar turned over eight times in our community just on building our house.

When the eight people who helped build our home buy goods in the community the dollar just keeps turning over in the community helping families to live a better life."

"So Dad, when you pay someone in the community to do work this help to build economic wealth?"

"Yes Son, and most important it helps to build pride. The dollar just keep on going from one hand to another hand in our neighborhood and that helps capitalism work for us.

Charles can you name some other ways the dollar turns over in our community?"

"I am thinking Dad." I then said, "We all buy groceries from Mr. Roscoe's Grocery Store."

"That's good Son, name some more," said Dad. "Daniel's dad cut our hair. Mom gets her hair styled at Mrs. Mae's Beauty Shop. Dr. Leroy is our family doctor and Dr. Jones is our Dentist. Oh yes, I almost forgot that we buy fresh fruits and vegetables from Mr. Sam's garden."

"Now Son do you understand how the dollar turn over in the neighborhood and keep the community strong?"

"Yes Dad, I do understand now and I understand how important that is."

"Dad, why were our teachers educated at Land-Grant College's?"

"Charles Land Grant Colleges are an important part of our educational development. They were built because Negro people are not allowed to attend State College's in many areas of the United States. The Land Grant Colleges educate over 80 percent of our Negro professionals. These Colleges are supported with State funds also.

Our neighborhood doctors, dentist, lawyers, teachers, architects, engineers, carpenters, plumbers and other professionals are degreed from Land Grant Colleges."

Mom closed the topic by saying, "Did you hear that old man Roberts died last night?" "Oh No!" Said Dad, "I will go over to the funeral home to see if I can help the family."

The funeral home owner was the richest man in our neighborhood. My mom says he got rich with all the insurance money he received to bury people. He owned a big colonial style brick house with tall columns in front. We would be afraid to go by his house because the funeral parlor was next-door. Our grandparents would tell us ghost stories so we were afraid of dead people.

"Hey Guys," Daniel said, "There is a wreath on Mr. Oliver's home. I wonder who is dead?"

"I don't know," said Percy, "but whoever it is they are lying in the casket in the front room."

We took off running as fast as we could.

It was a custom that when someone died, the body would be prepared by the funeral home and then put into a casket. The casket with body would be brought to the family home. The family would have friends and family to

31

come by and see the body. Some people would bring food for the family. The body remained at the home until the funeral was held at the church.

Some of the homes in our neighborhood were made with bricks and some were made with all wood.

My dad who was a skilled brick mason help build the brick homes. Many of these homes had green grass and shrubs.

Some of the wooden built homes were nice homes too. They had nice yards and little white picket fences.

But some of the homes were poorly built. After time they would tilt. It appeared as if they would fall apart.

My dad was a skilled builder, so I asked him, "Dad why do some of the homes have holes in the walls and the house dip and lean?"

Dad said, "Some of the wood built homes are not built by skilled carpenters. Some of the dads and moms did not have enough money to pay someone to build their homes. They could not afford to buy concrete to build a foundation for their homes. They also could not afford to buy lumber."

"If they could not afford to buy lumber, then what are the houses made from?"

"Son, they go out and find scrap lumber wherever they can find it and use this scrap lumber on building their home."

"But dad, what is holding the home up if not concrete?" I asked.

"They cut down a tree and cut it into stumps. The stumps are then used for the foundation on which they build their home. After time the stumps and scrap lumber will dry rot causing the house to slump. This causes a house to dip and tilt, Son."

"Dad, my friend, Percy's house is made like that."

"Yes Charles but I want you to know that there is a difference between a house and a home," said his dad. "Percy's mom has surrounded her family with a fine home."

"I don't understand dad. What is the difference between a house and home?"

"Son, a house can be made of brick, wood or scrap wood. It doesn't matter what it is made of. But a home is much more than just a structure. A home is the comfort of peace that surrounds you with love and joy. No matter where you go in the world, Son, you should always be able to look back at home as being like a mother earth to you."

"I never heard of a mother earth Dad. What is a mother earth?" I asked.

"Mother earth is generation's of arms around you and guiding you Charles. It is the love of your mom and I also guiding you and protecting you just as our parents did for us."

In the evening when it was cooler dad and I went for a walk in the neighborhood. He would point different things out to me and explain. We would stop and talk with most of the neighbors. Neighbors like our teachers, the minister, the principal, and Mr. Sam, the gardener.

Mr. Sam would always be in his garden pulling grass and watering. His garden looked the picture of fresh produce in a grocery store. The tomatoes were big and ruby red, and sweet as a plum. He would always give me one to eat. All his greens had large fluffy leaves. People would come from all over to buy from his garden.

"Watch out dad, here comes a truck."

"That truck will be stopping here son," said Mr. Sam. "My wife and grandchildren are on that truck.

They are coming from the cotton field. They must be some tired. They left here this morning at sunrise to go pick cotton."

The truck stopped in front of Mr. Sam's house and his wife and grandchildren climbed off the back of the truck.

Their face and arms were dark red from sun exposure. They had a scarf wrapped around their hair and on their head was a big straw hat.

"Good evening Mrs. Sam," said my father. "How are you and family today?"

"I am tired, son," said Mrs. Ledia Sam. "I picked 200 pounds of cotton today. I am so proud of my grandchildren. John picked 100 pounds of cotton for the first time and Mae picked 60 pounds."

"That's great Mrs. Sam," responded my father.

"How old are your grandchildren now?"

"John is 10 years old and Mae is 8 years old," said Mrs. Sam. "They have earned enough money this summer to buy their school clothes."

"How much do they pay these days for cotton picking?"

"They pay $1.50 per 100 pounds of cotton picked," Mrs. Sam responded.

"John how long have you been picking cotton?" I asked.

John said, "I started picking cotton at 5 years old."

Mrs. Sam said, "That's right, John was so small when I first took him to the cotton field. I made him a cotton sack from a crooker sack by sewing a strap on it. He was too small to pull a 5-foot long cotton sack."

Most of the children and elders picked cotton and chopped cotton to help the family with living expenses.

Mr. Sam's son, Jerry, worked at the sawmill. Jerry's wife, Wanda, worked as a maid at a hotel. Neither of them made very much money.

Dad and I completed our walk and returned home.

CHAPTER 7
GRANDMA'S VISIT

After doing my homework. Spike and I, came out to play with my can of marbles in hand.

The can was full of large and small marbles.

Spike and I went over to Daniel's home. I knocked on the door. His mom came to the door.

"Mrs. Williams can Daniel come out to play?" "Yes Charles, if he is finished with his homework," said Mrs. Williams.

Mrs. Williams called out to Daniel, "Daniel have you completed your homework?" Daniel answered, "almost mom."

"He will be out to play, Charles, when he finishes," said Mrs. Williams.

Spike and I left Daniel's home and went to Percy's house. I knocked on the door. No one answered. I knew that sometimes Percy had to help his mom with the laundry and that he could be in the back yard.

Spike and I went around to the back of the house. Percy was helping his mom take the dry clothes off the clothesline.

Some of the clothes were stiff with starch. His mom would dampen the starched clothes and roll them so they would be easier to iron.

"Hi Mrs. Julin, can Percy play with me?"

"Hi Charles," she said as she rubbed Spike on his head. "Hi, Mr. Spike, how is the good dog today?"

Mrs. Julin knew that Spike loved to be noticed. He would waggle his tail with approval for all the attention.

"Percy can play as soon as he is done helping me. You and Spike can wait for him. He will be finished soon," replied Mrs. Julin.

Percy called out, "Mom I am finish is there anything else?"

His mom replied, "No Percy, You can go play now."

Percy, Spike and I left to go play marbles.

Daniel had just finished his homework so he saw us out in front of his house. He called out to Percy and I, "Wait guys! I want to play marbles too."

Daniel's mom had scolded him about being on his knees and ruining his jeans.

Daniel said to his friends, "My mom will be angry with me if I get holes in the knees of my brand-new jeans. My grandma is visiting us from Annapolis. She bought us lots of new clothes. Grandma says the clothes cost her lots of money so we must take care of them.

"Percy, do you like for your grandma to hug and kiss you when she comes to visit?" Asked Daniel.

"No! No! No!" said Percy. "I like for her to hug me but not to kiss me. What about you Charles?"

"Me either," I said, "Grandma dips snuff, and she always has a big dip of snuff in her mouth when she want to kiss."

We laughed and laughed.

Daniel said, "yes and she always ask me to get her a can for her to spit the snuff in."

"Yes, I know," said Charles, "sometimes when I am not home she pours my marbles out and use my marble can to spit her snuff in. I don't like that."

"I know," said Percy, "but I love for my grandma to come visit us."

"Yes I do too," said Charles.

"My grandma cooks the best greens, chicken and dumplings, cornbread and my favorite bread pudding with lemon sauce. I love my grandma's cooking," said Percy.

"Hey man, this makes me hungry. Let's setup to play marbles."

"I will go and change quickly," said Daniel.

Daniel ran back into the house to change clothes. He could not find any knee torn jeans to play in.

"Mom," he called out, "where are my play jeans?"

His grandma heard him call out and said, "Daniel, grandma has patched all your jeans that were torn in the knees."

Daniel's mom did not have a sewing machine, but his Grandma did not care about that. Grandma would cut pieces from old jeans and patch holes in his torn jeans.

Grandma sewed on all the patches with her weak hands and fading eyesight.

Grandma's health was not good. She had High Blood Pressure and Sugar Diabetes.

She called his mom, Sis. She would say, "Sis thread this needle for me."

"The Sugar Diabetes is causing Grandma's eyesight to fade, that is why she can not see the hole in the needle." Daniel's mom said.

Daniel put on a pair of the patched jeans and ran back out to play marbles.

The boy's jeans always had patches in the knees. They played marbles everyday.

To shoot the marbles they had to get on their knees.

CHAPTER 8
A GAME OF MARBLES

Where we lived there were no parks where we could play. We looked for vacant lots to play football, baseball, Spinning-top and marbles. Before we could play we would have to clean the lot up first by removing the bottles, cans and other debris.

There was always someone's mom at home and they all looked out for the children.

Everyone's mom was a step-mom and every home was a second home.

Church was the central focus of our life.

All the children went to Sunday school. After Sunday school, we attended church with our parents.

Often on Sunday there would be a picnic on the church grounds for all the families to come. There would be fried

Chicken, honey cured ham from the smoke house, potato salad, greens, candied yams, red beans and rice, macaroni and cheese, cobbler with dumplings, butter pound cake, red soda water, and Aunt Susie's home made rolls. The food was so good. Most of the prepared food came from neighborhood gardens.

At these picnics is where we learned to play the game of marbles. All the children would gather around as we took turns playing the game of marbles.

After the picnic our famous marble game was played at home on the side of the street. Some days the marble game was played in the vacant lot when other children were not playing football or baseball.

The best time to play marbles in the street would be after the city came out and graded the streets.

There had been a big storm. The lightning was coming through the house like bright lights on a holiday. The lightning was striking with a loud cracking sound. You could hear it hitting the electrical transformers on the wood poles. The reflection would be like a bright rainbow. We would be so afraid. We would try to hide from the bright light the lightning made. Mom would say, "Turn all the lights out and get under the bed, hurry!"

The thunder would roar. The thunder would roar so loud that it would shake the house. Behind the loud thunder would come the crackling lightning. The rain would be pouring down so fast it sounded as if a jet airplane was hanging over our home.

We would be so afraid.

After the rain, the sandy dirt would create mud and ruts in the street. Cars and trucks would get stuck in the street.

My mom said, "The grader was here today and he graded 11th street," I said.

"Well the street is not as sandy as it was before the storm," said Daniel, "and the ruts and mud are gone. The crown is back on the street also."

"Charles, does your dad have a shovel?" asked Percy.

"Yes, I will go and get it."

I left and went to the back of my home. There in the back yard was a shed. These sheds were called, 'Junk

Houses'. These junk houses contained all of mom and dads stuff for the house.

Mom's stuff was canned peaches, pears, figs, tomatoes and vegetables from the summer garden.

There was also a big iron pot in the junk house that mom and dad would bring out. Then they would light a big fire under it and fill it with water.

The water would get hot, boiling hot. Then the water would be used for making soap, or boiling dirty clothes, or sterilizing the jars for canning.

We ate on the canned food all winter.

Dad's stuff in the junk house was yard and gardening tools, carpenter tools, hunting, and fishing gear.

Sometimes dad would hang meat that had been cured in the junk house.

There were no refrigerators.

We had an icebox. A big block of ice went into the top of the icebox. The cool air from the ice kept the food from spoiling.

Sometimes when we had no ice to cool the food, mom would rap the perishable food in a crooker sack. Then mom put the crooker sack in the water well bucket. Then she would lower the bucket deep into the well where it is cool. After that she would put the lid over the well for safety.

A crooker sack was made of burlap. Dried beans, rice and peanuts were sold in a crooker sack. The crooker sack when empty was then used to store food from the garden in the junk house.

I got the shovel from the junk house and went back to help prepare for the game of marbles.

After shoveling an area of loose sand, Percy said, "The area is smooth enough. Now lets dig the holes for the game."

Daniel found a rock on the side of the street.

"We can dig the holes with this rock," said Daniel.

Percy and I thought that was a great idea.

"I will dig the first hole," said Daniel.

"OK Daniel, but do not dig too big of a hole. Each hole has to be about two inches in diameter."

"OK!" said Daniel, "How about this hole it is about two inches across the center?"

"Yes that is good, now give me the rock I will dig the second hole."

"The third hole is mine," said Percy.

"Percy, your hole is not straight behind hole number two. each hole must be vertical to each other."

"Vertical?" asked Percy.

"What is Vertical?"

"My dad says a straight line that goes up and down is a vertical line."

"Gee, Charles," said Percy. "I never knew that."

"Let's play now," said Daniel.

"Hey Guys. Hold up. We can't play yet, we forgot to draw the start line."

"Percy, you have the biggest feet," said Daniel, "so you walk off the start line."

"Yeah, Percy walk ten vertical steps back from hole number 1. Now walk 6 horizontal steps across the top. Daniel will draw the horizontal line."

"Horizontal Line?" asked Daniel.

"What is a horizontal line, Charles?"

"Percy, just put one foot before the other for six steps overhead the holes. Daniel will draw a straight line directly overhead with the rock as you walk it off."

"Now we are ready to play."

"Who will go first, Charles?"

"We will all shoot the marbles from behind this start line to determine who will start."

"The start line is a horizontal line. The game holes are lined up vertical to the start line."

"We are now ready to play a game of marbles."

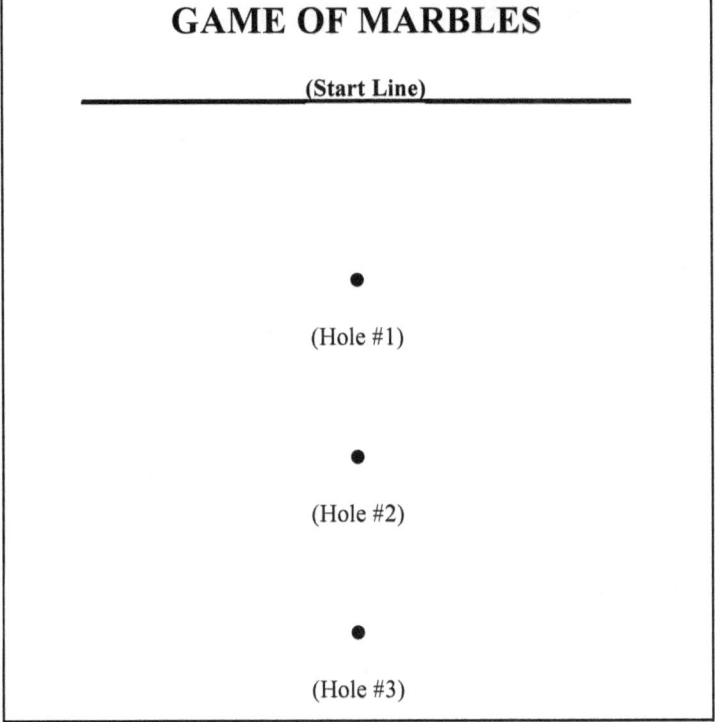

CHAPTER 9
PLAYING MARBLES

The marble game was played with great enthusiasm. It takes great skill to shoot the marbles and to become a winner.

Some players chose to play with large marbles and some chose small marbles.

Whatever marble you start out with you must continue to use that marble throughout the game.

I poured the marbles from the can onto the dirt.

"The beautiful blue marble is mine,"

"I want the sparkle red marble," said Percy.

"I love green," said Daniel, "so get back for the green."

To begin the game each player must lag a marble standing behind the first hole. A marble is lagged by tossing it gentle from the palm of your hand.

The marble that lands the closest to the start line will be the first shooter. The next closest marble to the line will be the second shooter.

"Now lets lag the marble to see who will go first."

"Let's all stand behind hole number 1,"

They all stood behind the first hole.

Daniel said, "I will lag first with this winning green marble." His marble landed a foot before the line.

"It's your turn now Charles," said Percy.

I remarked, "Get back, I will lag the winner."

I landed over the line.

Percy shouted! "It's my turn! Now keep your eyes on this winner."

He put the red marble in the palm of his hand and let the marble roll down his fingers and with a little push on the marble out it came. His marble landed almost on the line.

Percy shouted, "I won! I won! I will shoot first."

Daniel said, "I am the second shooter, Charles you are last."

"We will all shoot from behind the start line,"

At the start of the game all players must lag the marble into the first hole.

Percy tosses the first marble. His buddies shouted, "MISS! MISS! MISSssssss!"

It landed in the first hole.

Now the rules of the game change for the second hole.

To shoot for the second hole you must first span the hole area about 180 degrees with your thumb in the hole.

Percy put his thumb in the first hole, then he spread his fingers and spanned the area around the hole.

Percy now will shoot for the second hole from the spanned area. If he missed, the next shooter will lag for the first hole.

His buddies began to chant, "MISS! MISS! MISSssssss!"

Percy shot for the second hole. He missed.

Percy's red marble must stay at the position where he missed.

Now Daniel will lag the marble for the first hole.

His buddies began to chant, "MISS! MISS! MISSssssss!"

Daniel missed the first hole.

I will now lag the marble for the first hole.

His buddies began to chant, "MISS! MISS! MISSssssss!"

I tossed the marble and made the first hole.

His buddies began to chant louder, "MISS! MISSssssss!"

I began to brag, "Keep your eyes on this beautiful blue marble. It is hot!"

I shot for hole number 2 and made it.

"WOW!" Percy shouted. "He is hot."

Percy and Daniel are down on both knees. They are pounding on the ground. At the same time they are chanting "MISS! MISS! MISSssssssss the hole!"

"Are you looking," I bragged. "Watch this marble go all the way in the hole."

I shot for hole number 3 and made it.

The rules of the game now are once a shooter has shot and made all three holes he has to reverse the shooting.

The shot is now from hole number 3 to hole number 2.

I continue to brag, "Two more shots and I am out. Come on Mr. Blue Marble make the hole," he said.

Percy and Daniel are down on both knees. They are pounding on the ground. At the same time they are chanting "MISS! MISS! MISSssssssss the hole!"

I shot for the second hole and missed.

"Oh no!" I said, "well its your turn to shoot Percy."

Percy shot for the second hole and made it.

Now Daniel and I are chanting, "MISSsssss! MISS!" and hoping for Percy to miss the third hole.

Percy now began to brag. "Come on Mr. Red Marble don't let me down," he shouted, as he got down on one knee and put the red marble in position to shoot.

Daniel and I continued to chant. "MISSsssssss! MISSsssssss!"

Percy shot for the third hole and made it.

Now Percy must shoot in reverse. He had to make a choice. He could shoot at my blue marble that is sitting near the second hole or he can shoot for the second hole.

If Percy shoot for my marble and hit it, I must start over at hole number one.

Now, Percy must decide to shoot for the hole or for the blue marble.

Daniel shouted, "Shoot Charles' blue marble."

I shouted, "Shoot for hole number 2."

Percy decided to shoot for my blue marble, because it was close to hole number 2.

Percy got down on both knees. He looked at the position of the blue marble. He knows he must shoot the red marble at an angle to hit the blue marble.

The game is exciting now. His buddies are chanting and pounding on the dirt, "MISS! MISS! MISSsssssssssssss!"

Percy kissed his red marble and put it between his thumb and index finger and gave it a thump.

Out came the red marble.

BANG! It hit the blue marble.

"Oh no!" I shouted. "I have to start over." I picked up my blue marble and waited for Percy to shoot for the last hole.

His buddies began to chant over and over, "MISS! MISS! MISSsssssssss Percy!"

We really wanted Percy to miss now because he is shooting to go out.

Percy shot for the last hole and made it.

Percy is now out of the game.

Daniel and I both are at hole number 1.

It is Daniel's turn to lag the first hole.

The first one of us to finish all five holes is out.

So Daniel and I took turns shooting each hole. The game is tense now because no one wants to lose.

The chanting continued for each player to miss the hole.

Daniel's marble is now in reverse at hole number two.

My marble is also positioned at hole number two in reverse.

Daniel is the shooter. He has a choice to hit my blue marble and end the game or he can shoot for the last hole.

Percy shouted. "Hit Charles blue marble!"

I shouted. "Shoot for the hole!"

Daniel will now shoot to go out.

He thumped the marble and out it came, rolling fast and picking up speed as it rolled. The marble fell into the last hole.

"OH NO!" I screamed. "WHAT LUCK!"

"YES! YES! YES! You are the looser Charles."

The loser will have to put their knuckles over the first hole while the winner's shoot to hit their knuckles.

"WOW!" I said.

"Put your knuckles over hole number one Charles," said Daniel, "and I will shoot first to cool your knuckles down."

I put my knuckles down over hole number one.

Daniel got his green marble and with a big thump! He hit my knuckles.

I screamed, "Hay! That hurt."

Percy got his red marble and thumped it toward my knuckles. Percy thumped the red marble so hard that it jumped over my whole hand.

The game was over.

"Good game," I said as I began to gather up my marbles.

"Yeah!" said Daniel and Percy, as they help put the marbles back into the can.

The sun was going down so the boys left for home.

CHAPTER 10
CHARLES BEYOND 11TH STREET

Elementary school brought about changes in the life of each of the boys.

Walking home from graduation Charles' dad said, "Charles, I am so proud of you. I know you want to go to high school here in the city but your mom and I have selected a Preparatory school out of the state for you to attend."

"A preparatory school? Dad will I be able to play sports?"

His dad replied, "Yes Charles, you will attend

Paul Laurence Dunbar High School. This is a Negro Preparatory School, one of the best in the country."

"What sports do they have, Dad?"

"Son, you are going for the academics. If your grades do not suffer, you can play football, basketball, baseball or do field and track if you like."

I had never been away from home. I was a little frightened, but I didn't want my parents to know.

When summer ended I left for high school.

All the students were assigned to a counselor on the first day of school.

My counselor was Mrs. Green.

"Charles," Mrs. Green said, "this school prepares you for college. You will be required to do all homework assignments. You must make a grade of 'C' or better. Anything less and you will be dismissed from school. Do you understand?"

"Yes I understand," I said.

"Mrs. Green, I want to make time in my schedule to play sports."

"What sport would you like to play Charles?"

"I want to play football."

"Charles," Mrs. Green said, "I suggest that you not play your first year at school. You must first make good grades and then you can play sports."

I was not satisfied with this decision but I remembered what my dad had told me.

I made it through the first year with good grades. "Now I can play football." I said to myself. "I will go meet the coach."

I left for school a week early. This is my second year at school. I went to the football coach. "Coach, I want to be on the football team."

The coach asked, "What position do you play?"

"I have never played football coach but I am quick and I learn fast."

"How fast are you? Asked the coach.

"Well I am not sure Coach." The coach then said, "Run out 50 meters while I clock you." I ran as fast as I could.

The coach said, "Yes you are fast and with a little training you will get faster. You have made the team. You will be one of our wide receivers."

I trained often and became one of the best football players on the team.

The coach saw the athletic ability in me. Spring quarter the coach was putting together the track team. "Charles," he said, "I want you to join the track team." I had never participated in track, but I was excited about the coach asking me to join the track team.

"I never ran track before Coach. What will I run?" The coach said, "Charles you are fast. I want you to run the 200 meter and to be a long-jumper."

"Long-jumper? What is that Coach?"

"To long-jump you must run as fast as you can and then push yourself into the air while propelling yourself as far as you can in the air and land in a pile of sand. We will teach you how to do the long-jump Charles."

I had to practice extra to excelled in both sports. I played these sports with as much interest and enthusiasm as I played marbles. I knew to excel, I had to become competitive. My focus on track and field allowed me to become a Four-letter man.

Participating in these sports made me a great athlete but my grades began to suffer.

The famous letter came from my parents. "Charles," the letter stated, "how are your studies going? We want you to study harder, and we want to see the results reflected in your grades."

"WOW!" I said, "My parents are upset with me. I will find more time to study."

His parents watched his grades very closely. They kept reminding him that his main goal was to graduate with grades that could get him into college.

I began to put as much emphasis in my study as I had put into field and track. My grades improved. I earned a grade of 'A' in biology, chemistry and math. "When my parents see these grades, they will be proud of me. This will pull my grade point up." I said to myself.

I continued to play sports. I also found time to study and to make good grades for the remaining two years of high school.

All of my family came to graduation. When my name was called I went up on stage to receive my diploma. I also got a surprise.

The principal announced, "Charles is one of our best athletes and he is a great scholar. Charles you have earned a partial scholarship to Amherst College in Massachusetts."

I threw my arms up in the air and shouted, "YEAH! This is for you mom and dad." He shook the principal's hand thanking him and left the stage.

After graduation his dad said, "Charles we are proud of you. We knew you would be a good student and athletic. Thanks son for all your efforts. Amherst College will be a complete change from your high school." His dad continued, "There are very few people at Amherst that look like you son. You must keep your focus on your studies."

"I will do good dad. I love the game of sports also.

I want to play football and be on the track team."

I kept my word to my dad. I made good grades in my college classes and I joined the track team.

The track team attended a track meet at Brown University. After the meet the team were tired and hungry.

The coach said to the team, "You competed very well and I am proud of you. I will treat the team to dinner. I have made reservations for the team to enjoy a great dinner at Narragansett Hotel.

We were very excited about going to a hotel restaurant to eat. Most of the team had never eaten at a hotel restaurant. The team was also very hungry. This would be my first time just being at a large hotel. We all took showers and groomed our hair. We put on dress clothes. We boarded the bus excited about this treat.

The team arrived at the hotel. We entered the hotel lobby. The floor and walls of the hotel were a white with black accent marble. There was a large ruby red Oriental rug in the center of the floor. A huge chandelier with lots of bright sparkling crystal and lights hung from the center of the ceiling. All the customers in the lobby were white.

The doorman, the waiters and maids were Black.

The manager met the Coach and all the team in the lobby.

He had a friendly smile on his face. Shaking the coach's hand, he said, "Welcome to Narragansett Hotel."

The coach introduced himself and said, "we are the team from Amherst College and we have reservations for dinner."

The manager while looking over the team began to make eye contact with the Negroes. He stopped smiling and a troubling frown came upon his face.

He continued to focus his eyes directly at us when he said to the coach, "I am sorry coach but we do not serve colored people at this hotel. The white boys are welcome to eat here but the colored boys must go someplace else to eat."

Sue Blood Haynes, Ph.D.

The coach turned around to face the team but the team had all turned to leave the hotel.

The coach then said to the hotel manager, "If we cannot eat here as a team we will not be eating here."

The coach and the team left the hotel.

The team got back on the bus. The team was very silent on the ride back to campus.

That night I was so hurt. I felt violated. I tossed and turned in the bed. Why! Why! I said. What is this about? I pulled out a pencil and pad. I began to write my parents. "Mom and Dad, I am doing OK. I will graduate this summer with honors. I will apply for medical school. My goal is to become a medical doctor.

I am on the track and field team. I run the 200- meter and I also do the long jump. I am one of the best in both.

The ugly eye you warned me about has stared me in the face. Yes, it is different here just as you warned me. There are two Negroes on the track team. After a track meet at Brown University, our track coach planned for us to eat dinner at Narragansett Hotel. I was so excited about eating at a hotel. I wondered what the food would be like. Our team was very hungry.

The hotel would not seat us because some of us have a different skin color. I felt sad and hurt standing there in the hotel lobby, but my team mates made me feel better when they all turned and walked out of the hotel.

I also feel better now that I have written you."

I laid my head on the soft pillow and shut my eyes.

The next week I was in biology lab when the Dean entered the lab. He asked the instructor to get Charles. "Charles," he said, "I have a telegraph for you." The Dean gave the telegraph to me. It was from my parents. "Charles," the message read, "we have some sad news. Son, your dog Spike died today.

When your mom went out to feed him, he was lying still in the yard. She rubbed him on his head and he raised his head and barked three times and never moved again. Son he is gone. I will bury him in the back yard next to the junk house. Spike was 17 man-years old. That is a long life for a German shepherd dog. I am sorry Son about Spike."

I could not hold back the tears. Spike was my very best friend. I felt so lonesome. I left the class and went for a walk. While walking I thought of all the good times I had with Spike.

After the spring quarter ended I left for home on the train. My dad met me at the Train Station. "Dad, I miss Spike meeting me at the train. I miss him. I loved him so much. I made a tombstone for him. Let me show it to you." "A tombstone, son, let me see it." I pulled a wood carved plaque from my bag and handed it to my dad. Dad read aloud from the plaque. "To Spike the best friend I ever had. Love Charles."

CHAPTER 11
CHARLES CHALLENGE

The summer quarter was just about over and graduation is a near reality. I went to my counselor for assistance in applying for medical school.

The counselor said, "Charles, I need a photo to send with each application."

"Why do they require a photo Mrs. Griggs?" I asked.

"Charles," she said, "sending a photo and declaring race is often used to limit acceptance to medical school if you are of Negro decent."

"Should I declare Negro decent, Mrs. Griggs? Some people can't tell from my photo that I am Negro."

"Charles it is better to tell them you are Negro," said Mrs. Griggs. If they find out you are a Negro while you are in school they will expel you and you don't want that on your record."

I applied to over twenty medical schools. I met all the requirements listed on the application.

I went to the mailbox everyday hoping to get the acceptance letter.

"No! Not again." I would say, as I created a spitball with the rejection letters and shot hoops with them into the garbage can.

As I made the hoop into the garbage can I would say, "YEAH! This one is for you. I will not give up." I would never miss.

My parents kept my spirits high. They knew very few white medical schools accepted Negro students. My parents kept hope alive, they prayed that one school would come through for me.

They would write often saying, "Son you will get accepted to medical school. Just keep applying. Negro doctors are needed in our communities. We love you."

Weeks had gone by and all the letters I received brought the same message, "Rejected."

I kept my spirits and hope alive by writing my thoughts in a diary. I continued to go to the mailbox everyday.

This day a letter was in the mailbox from McGill University in Montreal, Canada. Canada had always extended a warm hand to Negro people. Many slaves fled the United States to Canada for freedom.

All the right words were on the letter from McGill University, "You have been accepted into our five-year medical school program...," I read aloud. I was so excited. I leaped into the air with my arms stretched out and shouted, "Yeah! Yeah! Yes! Here it is!"

79

I ran into the house, gathered all my clothes, books and belongings and boarded the train for Canada.

I made my studies a priority at medical school. I also made time for the track and field team.

Medical school required a lot of study. My classmates could not understand how I found time to include sports in my schedule. To play sports in medical school is rare and difficult. My classmates asked, "Charles where do you find time to play sports? Our classes and medical work is so demanding. We have very little free time."

"Sports are my second love. The exercise I receive is good for my body as well as my mind. Exercise keeps my mind fresh which helps me to study."

"This guy is unbelievable," his classmate said to his peers. "Charles is an honor student in medicine. He is a great athletic. I was at his track meet when he won medals in high and low hurdles and the long jump. I don't know how he does it."

CHAPTER 12
EXPERIENCING SUCCESS

I often thought about my childhood friends and how we loved to played marbles. "I miss the game of marbles, that was my first love of sports."

One of my professors, Dr. John Beattie, from Great Britain, was conducting research on blood. I thought this was a fascinating area of research. I wanted to be part of the research on blood. I read all available materials I could find on blood.

One day after class Dr. Beattie approached me. He said, "Charles you are a great student. You are smart and I admire the scholar in you. I want you to join my team in the research of blood."

I was fascinated by this offer, I wanted to be part of this research on blood with Dr. Beattie.

"Dr. Beattie," I said, "I take my studies very seriously. I want to become a medical doctor one day. I am dedicated to hard work and study to become a doctor. I am interested also in the research of blood. I have read all available materials on the subject. I gladly accept your offer."

Dr. Beattie and I became very close and we continued research on how we could transfer blood from one person to another. We put extra interest on the research for the storage of blood to be later used during an emergency.

I saw people lose their lives from not having access to blood.

I was called on as a student to give fresh blood to save a life.

Once after a transfusion I approached my research partner and said, "Dr. Beattie I am concerned that hospitals must rely on fresh blood. We must find a way to store blood for emergencies."

I soon graduated from McGill College with a degree in Medicine and a Master's Degree in Surgery. I knew I had to complete my residency requirement in Canada. Hospitals in the United States were segregated. Separate hospitals for Negroes were few to none. Very few hospitals accepted Negro doctors for residency.

A residency requirement was necessary to watch and learn from an experienced doctor. Negro Doctors had to do house calls with few places to take their very sick patients.

After completing my residency in Canada, I wrote my parents, "Mom and Dad I have completed all requirements here in Canada. I am now a medical doctor. I would like to return to the United States."

My parent's letter back to me was gloomy.

"Son, the United States is in a financial depression. The stock market has crashed. Lots of people are without money and jobs. Poor people are on the verge of starvation. Some of the Negro people in the North and South are starving because they are being excluded from some of the soup kitchens. Soup lines are everywhere to relieve suffering.

If you can work in Canada, perhaps you should remain there for a while." My dad wrote.

I wrote back, "Dad what about the availability to hospitals. Are the hospitals still segregated?"

"Son," my dad wrote. "Your mom and I fear going to the hospital even for minor surgery. Most surgical patients die from infection that set in after surgery. Disease in the hospital's is not adequately controlled."

"Dad, I must return home, I can see where my people need me."

I was home sick. I gathered all my belongings and returned to the United States. I was hired as a surgical teacher at Howard University, a Negro University in Washington D.C., and as an assistant surgeon at Howard University's Freedman Hospital.

I continued blood research efforts. I also continued to see more and more people die due to the lack of available blood. This caused me to push blood research for more answers.

"I need a science degree to do more in-depth research on Plasma, the fluid of blood," I said to the Head Surgeon. "But where can I go? No White University has accepted Negroes in a Doctorate of Science Degree program. I must find another way to be accepted"

The Head Surgeon said, "Charles, I was told that Columbia University in New York is offering a two year scholarship to doctors. You should apply."

I remembered how difficult it was applying to medical school in the United States. With some reluctance, I decided to apply and was accepted. "What a great opportunity," I said to the Head Surgeon. "Now I can work on a Doctor of Science Degree. I can do medical research on blood plasma

at the Presbyterian Hospital while I attend school. WOW!
This is the break I needed."

CHAPTER 13
REACHING OUT

I completed the requirements for a Doctor of Science Degree. My final paper for the degree was a Dissertation entitled, 'Banked Blood: A Study in Blood Preservation.'

I wrote Dr. Beattie. He had returned back to Great Britain.

"Dr. Beattie, I have made a medical discovery on the research of blood plasma. The results are documented in a 245-page Dissertation that I wrote for a Doctor of Science Degree. In the research I discovered that by drying blood plasma it could be stored for later usage. Mix water with the dry blood plasma and the result is liquid blood for medical emergencies.

I also explain how to setup blood banks in the document."

Dr. Beattie excited about this discovery, responded. "Charles, your medical breakthrough has come just in time. We need your help. Our troops are fighting in World War II. Germany is at war with Great Britain. Thousands of our troops are being wounded and are in needed of blood to survive. Please help by sending blood plasma from the United States."

I could not let my friend down. I started a campaign by advertising in newspapers, "Please help, come and give your blood to the 'Blood for Britain' program." I set up a blood bank.

Over 14,500 people responded and gave blood for the program.

I set up a system to dry the blood. The dry plasma was then shipped to Dr. Beattie for the wounded soldiers.

The Red Cross became interested in this new discovery of Blood Plasma. My research had proven to be successful. They knew of my heroic act of sending blood plasma to Great Britain. The Red Cross contacted me and said, "Charles you have proven that blood plasma can be stored. We want to set up blood banks. We need you to help us"

My dream was finally becoming a reality. The dream to install blood banks all over the United States and the world. I agreed to assist the Red Cross in the installation of Blood Banks.

The Red Cross gave me the title of Assistant Director over Blood Banks. One day while observing blood plasma being dried, I asked the nurse, "Why do you have two separate rooms for storing blood plasma?"

The nurse answered, "One room is for blood taken from white people and the other room is for blood taken from colored people."

I explained to the nurse, "There is no medical reason to separate the blood. Blood taken from Negroes is the same as blood taken from whites."

I was annoyed by this procedure. I was assured that the orders came from the head of the Red Cross.

I contacted the head of the Red Cross with my concerns and complaint on separating the blood.

I said to the Director, "Separating blood of whites and Negroes are medically incorrect. Blood has nothing to do with color. There are four main blood types, A, B, AB, and O.

The type 'O' person can supply blood to all groups. The type 'AB' person can receive blood from all types. The color of a person's skin has nothing to do with blood type."

The Red Cross did not agree with me.

They responded, "We will continued to segregate blood of whites and blacks. We believed that if whites used blood plasma taken from blacks their skin color would change."

I became frustrated with this decision and left the Red Cross.

I returned to working with students and the hospitals.

"Dr. Drew," a peer physician said, "I am concerned about your health. You are in the hospital most of the time. When do you sleep?"

"I manage some sleep. The Doctor's in residency need my assistance and advice. I must be around for that."

"Dr. Drew are you going to the Medical Conference that starts tomorrow?" Asked one of the physicians.

"Yes, I am making a presentation at the conference."

"Perhaps we can share the ride to the conference. I will drive" "Yes, that will be ok," said Charles, "but I will drive."

The next day I prepared for the trip with the three Physicians. The other physicians wanted to drive but I insisted on driving. We had to travel about two hundred miles for the Medical Conference. Preparing over the night for my speech, I had very little sleep, but I insisted on driving.

The loud talk and music was not enough to keep me from falling asleep at the wheel.

The men in the car screamed out, "Watch it Charles." As the car dashed across both lanes of the highway, jumped a ditch, rolled over and hit a tree. One of the Doctor's was not seriously hurt. He called out, "Dr. Drew are you ok?" I could hear him but I could not answer. I could not move. I was seriously hurt. The Doctor had a neighbor to call for an ambulance.

I was loosing lots of blood. The ambulance came to get Dr. Drew. The medic's said, "Where will we take him? There are no Negro hospitals close. He can't go to a white hospital. They will not accept him."

The Doctor said, "He need immediate medical attention and he need a blood transfusion."

"Sorry," said the medic's person, "You can use my ambulance to operate, but where will you get the blood?"

Dr. Charles Drew became weaker and soon lost complete consciousness. He had loss so much blood and he needed a blood transfusion to save his life. He died later on the scene.

Daniel was notified of Charles death.

At Charles funeral Daniel spoke softly. "Dr. Charles Drew, my friend, made medical breakthroughs by discovering that blood can be dried. The blood plasma can be stored. The blood plasma can later be mixed with water and used for blood transfusions. His dedication to research became a reality. Dr. Charles Drew died because he could not go to a hospital and receive medical attention and receive a blood transfusion. However, my friend Dr. Charles Drew left a legacy for all mankind to receive stored blood plasma in the preservation of life. Goodbye Friend!

WOW!"

Daniel left the funeral with a heavy heart as he walked slowly to the Train Station. He boarded the train to return to Chicago. He sat quietly in the train boxcar marked for Colored People only. He lifted his eyes to the bright blue sky and said, "Why?" He began to reflect back on his childhood and the days on 11th Street with Charles and Percy. The train began to move swiftly. Daniel closed his eyes as visions of his past flashed in his memory.

CHAPTER 14
DANIEL BEYOND 11TH STREET

Daniel came to his father's barbershop everyday after he and his friends walked home from school.

"Dad," Daniel asked, "I want to become a barber. Can you teach me?" His dad answered,

"When business is slow Daniel, I will teach you."

Daniel was excited about learning the skill. He ran from school everyday for training. One day he entered into the barbershop. He found his dad bent over coughing very strong. He ran up to his dad patted him on the back and said, "Dad what's wrong?"

His dad said, "Son, I am not well. The weather here does not agree with me. This cough is getting so bad I feel we must move."

"Move!" Daniel said. "But where will we go?"

"We are going to Grandma Price's home in Annapolis," said his father.

"Is everyone going dad?" Daniel asked.

"Everyone is going Daniel," his father answered.

His father had the most successful and largest barbershop in town.

"What will happen to the barber shop Dad and our home?" Daniel asked.

"I will lease the barber shop Son and I will rent the house. When I get better we will return."

It was not very long before the family moved to Annapolis into Grandma Price's home.

Grandma Price had once been a slave in Maryland.

Grandma Price lived in a 4-bedroom home. She had a large yard with tall pine trees and a small vegetable garden.

The house had a large porch that spanned across the front of the house. On the porch was a chair swing that Daniel enjoyed sitting in with his grandma. Grandma would let the swing move slowly as she shared family history with Daniel. Daniel enjoyed talking with Grandma Price about history.

While still swinging Daniel asked his grandmother, "Grandma Price how did you get free?"

"Your grandfather, Henry Price, bought me out of slavery," she said.

"Your grandfather," she said, "was never a slave. He was a real estate contractor and a Methodist preacher. Your grandpa owned lots of real estate. He also made money through investing on the stock market. He used some of his profits to buy slaves into freedom. He was a wonderful man."

Making a home life in Annapolis was becoming more difficult as the father's health continued to decline. His coughing became worse.

Daniel asked, "Grandma why does dad cough so much?"

Grandma Price said, "Daniel your father has Tuberculosis which makes him cough."

"Will he ever get better?" Daniel asked.

"I am afraid not," said Grandma Price.

His father's coughing got worse, and this illness soon caused his death.

Daniel was so sad that his father had died. He became very depressed.

His mother, who had been married to his dad since she was eighteen years of age, felt very lonesome. She missed her husband. He took care of all the business for the family.

Early in the morning Daniel sat with his grandmother in the swing. He had not slept all night.

His grandma said, "Daniel what's wrong?"

"Grandma, my heart is paining. I hate to see my mother so sad. Why is she so sad, Grandma?" He asked.

"She is lonesome Daniel. Your dad is gone and she does not know how to provide for the family."

"But you are here Grandma and we are here too for her," said Daniel.

"Your dad left the family financially stable," said Grandma Price, "but he left your mom totally unprepared to manage the family affairs. He never discussed the details of the family's financial investments with your mother."

Daniel's mom joined them on the porch.

"Mom," Daniel said. The bill collectors are calling. Have you paid the bills?"

"I do not know where all the investments are," said his mom. "I do not have any money."

"Let me help?" asked Daniel.

"I can't," said his mom, "I do not know where to start. Your dad did not share the business and investments with me."

Daniel became even sadder because his mom was so depressed she could not manage the family either.

"What will happen to our family Mom?" Daniel asked.

His mom answered, "I can't hold the family together any longer Daniel. I feel so sad. I must separate the family." "How will we be separated mom?"

His mom answered, "Price will go to live with cousins in New York.

Sally and Ann will go to Chicago to live with our cousins.

Ida and Alice will stay here with Grandma Price."

"What about me mom, where will I go?" Daniel asked. His mom looked at him very sadly and said, "Daniel you know Mr. Mason, your dad's friend?" she asked. "Yes mom," Daniel answered. "Well, he has a shoemaking school in Baltimore. You will live with him while you learn shoemaking."

Daniel was very sad as he asked, "Mom where will you go?"

She answered, "I will go to Chicago with your sisters to live with our cousin also."

Daniel lowered his head. Put his hands into his pockets. With tears in his eyes, he walked away slowly.

Daniel left to live with the shoemaker.

He attended classes for shoemaking. "I am not interested in shoemaking," Daniel would say to himself. "I will leave as soon as I can."

Shoemaking reminded him of days back in his hometown. There he had to cut cardboard to put into his shoe to cover holes in each shoe sole.

Mr. Mason treated Daniel like his own son, but Daniel was not happy because he missed his family.

One day Mr. Mason left to go and pick up more supplies for shoe making. Daniel said to himself, "today is the day, I am leaving for Chicago to be with my mom and sisters."

Daniel ran to the train station. He knew the train would be pulling into the station about a half pass noon.

The ticket man at the train station had been a friend of his father.

He ran up to the ticket man and said, "Mr. Olson! Please sir! I have no money, but I need a ticket to visit my mom in Chicago!"

Mr. Olson could see the desperate look in Daniel's eyes so he gave him a ticket.

Mr. Olson said to Daniel, "Make sure you sit in the car marked for Colored People. You will get put off the train if you sit in the car marked for White's only."

The train came and Daniel left for Chicago. He was afraid because he had never traveled alone.

The train stopped at every town. "OH no! This train is not stopping again," he thought. "Where is this?"

The train was stopping for some people on the railroad tracks out in the country.

While traveling Daniel was hungry but he was afraid to go to the dining car. He asked the colored woman sitting next to him, "Can Negro people go to the diner to eat?"

"The diner is for white people child," she said. "If you are hungry just tell the Porter what you want. He will bring you something to eat."

Daniel asked, "How much does the food cost?"

She answered, "Too much, Son. Just tell the Porter you are hungry, and he will get the cook to bring you some food after the diner closes. All the cooks are Negro, just like the Porter."

While Daniel was sleeping the elderly lady told the Porter to bring Daniel some food. It was late and he felt someone shaking him, "Son, wake up?" Daniel awaken to find the cook standing over him with a bag of food. "Thanks," Daniel said to the cook. "I am very hungry and I only have a dime in my pocket."

"Keep the money," he said, "enjoy the food."

The train finally arrived in Chicago. The train station was huge, with lots of trains and lots of people. Daniel finally found the exit sign.

He went up to a taxi driver and showed him his mom's address, "Sir can you take me to this address?" He asked. "Yes," he said, "that will cost you one dollar and fifty cents."

"My mom will pay," Daniel said to the taxi driver.

Daniel was hoping his mom would be home and not be angry with him.

The taxi arrived at his cousin's home. Daniel ran up to the house and knocked on the door. His mom came to the door. She was so happy to see him. She hugged and kissed Daniel and then she paid the taxi driver.

CHAPTER 15
CAREER CHOICE

Life for Daniel in Chicago became a challenge. He attended high school during the day and worked evenings as a barber to help support his needs.

Walking home from graduation exercises his mother said, "Daniel, I miss mother and your younger sisters. I have decided to return to Annapolis."

Daniel enjoyed being back with his mother and now she was leaving again. "Mother," he said softly, "I will miss you, I love you and my sisters but I will stay in Chicago.

"What will you do son?"

"I will look for a full time job as a barber. Please do not worry about me."

When Daniel's mother left Chicago, he had no job and only two dollars in his pocket. The only skill he had was cutting hair.

Daniel read in the Newspaper that a barbershop in nearby Janesville was looking for a full time barber.

He got dressed in his only suit and necktie. He walked to the train station and paid one dollar for a train ticket to Janesville.

When the train entered Janesville, Daniel did not know which way to go. He called out to the taxi driver, "Sir," he asked while holding the wanted aid paper in his hand. "Can you help me with directions to this barber shop." The cab driver pointed out the directions to Daniel.

He kept the directions in his memory and began to walk to the barbershop.

He entered the barbershop and said, "Hello, I am Daniel William's. I am seeking work as a barber."

A tall colored man greeted him and said, "I am Charles Anderson, the owner." Mr. Anderson extending his hand for a handshake and said, "I will show you around."

Mr. Anderson took Daniel to a room that had four long tables. Each table was covered with white sheets and a pillow. Each table was located in the room for privacy. Different color curtains separated the tables. The curtains were neatly folded with a tie band.

"This is the massage room," he said. Daniel had never heard of a massage. His eyes grew big as he asked, "What is a massage, Sir?"

Mr. Anderson called out, "Neal, could you come please?" a short Negro man entered the room.

"This is Daniel, could you demonstrate a five minute massage on him?" Neal said to Daniel, "Please pull your shirt off. Now lie on the table face down." Daniel pulled off his shirt and got onto the table face down.

Neal then said to Daniel, "Just relax your body."

Neal began to rub and tap Daniel's muscles in his back, arms and neck.

Daniel's back and neck muscles had never felt so good.

"This is so relaxing," said Daniel. "How long is a full massage?" Neal answered, "From thirty minutes to an hour. Whatever the client needs"

Daniel got off the table and was shown the next room, which was a hot steam bath room.

Mr. Anderson said, "This room is the final room the patrons enter before leaving. We have many different herb baths."

"The people who come here must be rich," said Daniel. "Yes," said Mr. Anderson, "most of the white businessmen from Chicago come here."

Daniel was so impressed. He wanted Mr. Anderson to know he wanted this job.

He said, "Mr. Anderson, I am a good barber. My dad was a barber and he taught me all there is to know about the trade. I am a good worker. I come to work early and I stay late."

Mr. Anderson looked at Daniel and said, "I like your attitude Daniel. Yes you have the job. When can you start?" Daniel answered, "Tomorrow sir!"

"Where are you living in town?"

"I must find someplace in town to live," said Daniel. Mr. Anderson replied, "You can live with my family."

Daniel moved in with the Anderson family. All the members of the family liked Daniel. They liked him so much that soon they treated him as if he was a member of the family.

Dr. Henry Palmer, a medical doctor, was one of the patrons that often came to the salon. Daniel became his barber and got to know him very well.

Daniel had learned that Dr. Palmer was one of the best physicians in the region. Dr. Palmer talked about how he was struggling to save a patients life that had been shot.

"Being a doctor is exciting," thought Daniel. "That is what I want to become," he said to himself. "I want to become a medical doctor."

He gave Dr. Palmer a visit at his large western style colonial red brick home.

He knocked on the door with the large lion head door-knocker located in the center of the door.

Dr. Palmer came to the door. "Can I help you young man," he said.

"Dr. Palmer I want to become a doctor," Daniel said. "It will be an honor sir, if you allow me to study under you."

The doctor only knew Daniel as a barber, not as a serious young man who had interest in becoming a doctor.

Dr. Palmer invited Daniel into his home. "Sit down young man," he said. "Do you know what it takes to become a medical doctor? "No," said Daniel, "I was hoping to work under you and learn to become a doctor."

"Daniel," the doctor said, "there was a time when you could serve an apprenticeship under a medical doctor and become a doctor. Times have changed. You must study medicine in College now and get a Medical Degree." Daniel looked up at him with sadness in his eyes. Dr. Palmer saw this sadness in his eyes and said, "Daniel, I will allow you to work under me and if you work hard I will help you to get into a medical college."

Daniel was excited about this offer. He quit his job as a barber and became a medical assistant to the doctor.

Daniel came to the doctor's office very early the next morning. Dr. Palmer greeted him and said, "Daniel over here is all my medical books. I want you to begin to read them to become familiar with medicine."

"I will read everyday," said Daniel.

"You will be responsible for keeping the records and to drive the horse buggy on house calls."

Daniel responded, "Yes Sir."

There was no hospital in Janesville so doctors made house calls for all illness, broken bones and amputations.

"Daniel," Dr. Palmer said, "You have been with me about a year. I believe you are ready to assist in your first amputation of a leg."

Being a barber, his skills with cutting became valuable in assisting the doctor.

"I am ready to assist," Daniel said.

Daniel began assisting Dr. Palmer more and more in repairing broken bones and amputations.

Pain killing medicine was rare. Dr. Palmer would say to Daniel, "Hold the patient down Daniel and do not allow him to move while I cut his leg off." Daniel got good at holding the patient down and that was no easy job.

Daniel became very excited about the work he was doing with Dr. Palmer and he knew that being a medical doctor was his dream. Now he was ready for medical school.

Dr. Palmer helped Daniel complete his application to Chicago Medical College. This school was one of the best training centers in the nation.

Dr. Palmer's son, Will Palmer, had graduated from there.

Dr. Palmer and Daniel was making a house call when Dr. Palmer said, "Daniel, I have some good news. You have been accepted at Chicago Medical College. And the good part is your tuition and fees will be paid."

"That is great news, Sir" said Daniel. "I will work hard and I will graduate."

Daniel was excited about the chance to go to medical school.

His excitement soon turned to sadness as his thoughts gathered. "I have no money. Where will I stay? And how will I eat?" The first person he wrote was his mother to share his excitement and to seek funds.

"Mother," he wrote, "I have been accepted to Chicago Medical College. I need money for room and board. Mother please help me? Please cash some of the stocks dad left. I will pay you back when I become a doctor."

Mrs. William's wrote Daniel back and said, "Son, I can't cash in stocks. I am sorry. The risk of school is too great. Write a family friend, Mrs. John Jones, in Chicago, and ask her to let you board in her home."

Grandma Price had died so Daniel could not turn to her for help.

Daniel wrote his working sisters and brothers. "Please help me! I have no money. I have been accepted into medical school. I have no place to live in Chicago while I attend school. Can you send me some money?" The answer came back the same, "Sorry Daniel, We have no money. We are struggling too."

Enrollment for fall quarter was only a month away and Daniel still had no place to live or money.

Desperate now to find boarding, he wrote Mrs. John Jones and said, "Mrs. Jones, I will be attending school at Chicago Medical College. I need a place to live while attending school. Can I board at your home?" "Come see me in Chicago," she answered.

Determined to become a medical doctor, he would not give up.

Daniel put the few clothes he owned with some other personal belongings in a white and brown-stripped cotton flour sack. He left for the train station.

After the biscuits were cooked and the chicken floured for frying, the empty flour sack served many purposes.

People would shop for flour by the pattern on the sack. Matching sacks were used for pillowcases.

Some of these cotton flour sacks were used to make dresses for girls and shirts for the boys. Most women knew how to sew. The clothes made from flour sacks were the only clothes most children knew or had.

CHAPTER 16
Vanishing Dream

The train ride to Chicago seemed longer than usual for Daniel. He had no money. "I hope Mrs. Jones will let me stay in her home." He said to himself. "What will I eat? I have got to find a way. This is my big chance."

Upon arriving into Chicago, Daniel had only a dime in his pocket.

He had to get to Mrs. Jones' home. With so little money in his pocket, Daniel had only one means of transportation, his feet.

He walked carrying the flour sack with his belongings for many miles to reach Mrs. Jones home.

Daniel finally arrived at Mrs. Jones home. He was so tired, "WOW! I am finally here."

There stood her home it was a sight of beauty.

Mrs. Jones lived in a rich neighborhood. There were only two homes on each block. Her house was a two story red brick house. The yard had manicured shrubs with deep green grass. There was a three-tier water fountain that gave a peaceful sound as the water flowed down each tier.

Mr. Jones was deceased. He was a real estate contractor that built their home.

Daniel did not want Mrs. Jones to know that he had no money to pay for boarding. He wanted to appear as if he was not so poor.

He sat his belongings down. He pulled down on the suit coat of his one and only navy blue suit. He straightened his necktie that he wore with a white shirt. "I hope Mrs. Jones accepts me," he said. He knocked on the front door.

Mrs. Jones came to the door. Before he could say anything she asked, "You must be Daniel Williams?"

"Yes, I am," replied Daniel.

"Come in child," she said. "You look just like your father."

Her home was furnished very nice with furniture. The entrance hall had a Grandfather Clock standing next to a mirror that went from floor to ceiling.

"And so you are going to Chicago's Medical College?" she asked.

"Yes, Mrs. Jones," Daniel said, "I will start this quarter. I need a place to board."

Mrs. Jones was checking out his looks, speech and manners, as she looked him straight in his eyes.

"You can stay here Daniel," she said, but I will not tolerate any visitors."

"I graciously accept," said Daniel, "I will obey your rules."

Daniel took his sack and followed Mrs. Jones to the room he would call home while in school.

"The only thing I need now is money," he said to himself, as he looked out the window from his bedroom. "I will write the Anderson's. They are my only real family. They have always helped me."

Daniel sat down and wrote a letter to the Anderson's explaining his situation.

"I have been accepted into Chicago Medical College. The school pays my tuition and books. I have no money for room and board. Can you send me some money?" wrote Daniel.

Mr. Anderson wrote Daniel back and sent him some money. The Anderson family was so pleased that he was in medical school.

"We are so proud of you Daniel being accepted into medical school. We can't send very much money Daniel, but we will send some money each month to help you out," wrote Mr. Anderson.

Daniel was so pleased to get the letter and the money.

Daniel studied often to make the best grades possible. He studied all the time. He spent most of his time from the library to the classroom. He was one of the top students in the class.

Daniel was thin and his lack of a full meal caused him to be even thinner. He still had money problems. He did not want to work, because work would take away from his study time. He wanted to make the best grades.

With the little money the Anderson's would send each month, he first paid Mrs. Jones for his room.

He would then buy a loaf of bread, a jar of peanut butter and a can of Brer Rabbit Molasses. Each day he made a peanut butter and molasses sandwich and this would be his only meal.

It was winter quarter and Daniel had been feeling a little ill but he ignored the symptoms. "I am so exhausted," he said, "but I must continue to study."

One day he collapsed at school.

Dr. Marcus Hatfield, his Chemistry teacher, hastened to his side to examine him.

"Daniel," he said, "How long has you been ill?"

"Not long," said Daniel.

"You have a temperature of 102 degrees," said the teacher.

The teacher was concerned because a smallpox epidemic had broken out.

"Your symptoms resemble the smallpox disease," said the professor.

Daniel was concerned because he remembered the polio epidemic. His best friend, Percy, who lived next door to him on 11th street contracted polio. He had a fever of 102 degrees. Percy was put into isolation from everyone in his home and community. Charles and I his best friends, could not visit him.

A man from Public Health quarantined his home. The spray used was so strong we could smell it at our house.

We would go to his bedroom window and call out, "Percy! Percy! Its us Charles and Daniel." Percy would slowly sit up in bed and give us a slow wave. "When can you come out to play marbles?" We would ask.

Percy would just stare as if he could not talk.

We would take turns getting on top of tin cans everyday and wave at our friend, Percy. He would be so glad to see us. He soon became cripple and very sick. No one could help him.

One day we heard his mom cry so loud that no one could console her.

Charles and I ran to Percy's window, got on top of the tin cans so we could look into his room. We saw the doctor pull the sheet over Percy's head. We knew we had loss our best friend. We sat under his window and cried until the hearse came and took Percy away.

CHAPTER 17
SUCCESS

Daniel was so frightened, "What if it is the smallpox. What will I do?" He said to himself. "I have no family in Chicago. I can't let the Anderson's down. I want to become a doctor. I can't let myself down."

Dr. Hatfield came into his room. "Daniel," he said, "the test results are back. "I am pleased. You do not have smallpox. You have Varioloid, an illness that resemble smallpox."

Daniel was pleased of the results but he was still very ill. He was too ill to attend classes. His grades suffered during the winter quarter. This brought his grade average down.

Daniel worked even harder spring quarter. "I must make better grades." He would say to himself. "I will lose my funding at school if my grades suffer any more." Daniel spent all his spare time catching up on what he had missed while ill. He succeeded in putting his grades back on target.

Daniel moved back to the top student in his class.

The semester was now over. It was exam time.

"Here are all my notes from all my classes," said Daniel applauding himself.

"Somehow it all seems easy to me now. I am ready for the final exams."

To become a doctor he had to prepare to complete a final written exam and an oral exam. "The oral exam will be the hardest," he said to himself. "I don't know what questions they will ask me. I must be prepared for any question."

Daniel knew most of the doctors that would be on the panel, like the head doctor of the hospital, three of his teachers and a doctor from the community.

Daniel was nervous. He could not eat. He could not sleep. He dreamed of the exam. Now the day was here. "This is it," Daniel said. "All my hopes and dreams will begin or end with these exams." He left for school.

Daniel's hard work and study as a student paid off. He answered successfully all questions on the written exam. On the oral exam he never stuttered. He knew every answer. "I feel so good." he said to himself, "I know the answers. I am ready to become Dr. Daniel Hale Williams."

After the last question on the oral exam, Daniel knew he had passed. All the doctors shook his hand. Daniel left the room and threw his hands up in the air as he jumped up and screamed, "YES! YES! I DID IT!" Daniel felt free. The clouds were gone. He could see clear sky. His whole life flashed before his eyes. It was a good feeling.

He did not wait for the results. He wrote Dr. Palmer. He wrote Mr. Anderson. He wrote his family. He wrote Charles. "Please come to graduation," he said, "I have finished all the requirements to graduate as a medical doctor."

Daniel made Chicago his home and started a practice there.

Mrs. Jones had many friends. She spread the word, "Come to Dr. Daniel Williams," she said, "He is a good doctor." He had lots of patients.

The hospitals in Chicago were segregated. Daniel had no hospital to take his patients. There were few Negro Nurses.

There was no school in Chicago that would accept Negro women to get nurse training. They could not attend the nurse training school in Chicago because of their color.

Daniel being a tall thin and gracious young doctor was of interest to many young women.

"Daniel," said Emma, one of his dates, "I came to Chicago looking to become a nurse. There are no nursing schools that will accept me because I am Negro."

Daniel replied, "There are no hospitals either in Chicago that will accept Negro doctors for residency practice after graduation.

"Can you do something about that Daniel? All the doctors here respect you and your work as a doctor."

Daniel began talking up the need for a hospital with a nursing school to community leaders.

He called a meeting with some engineers, architects, builders and some people with money.

"We need to plan a hospital with a nursing school," he told them.

"This will be a hospital for Negroes but it will not be a Negro hospital. It must be an institution of interracial good will. We will train all the nurses, technicians and interns at this facility."

The architect stood up and said, "Lets start a fund raiser for this hospital."

Chicago's millionaires, business people and individuals joined the fund-raising campaign. Money began to flow in.

"What will we call the hospital," said Daniel.

It was agreed that the new hospital would be called,

'Provident Hospital and Training School for Nurses.'

On opening day of the Provident Hospital and Training School for Nurses, Dr. Daniel Hale Williams told the audience, "This hospital is the first interracial hospital in America and we are proud of our committee's accomplishment here in Chicago."

CHAPTER 18
Being First

Chicago was proud of their new hospital. It was busy everyday. Daniel and staff performed over two hundred surgeries by the end of the first year.

A call sounded out in the hospital. "Calling Dr. Williams! Dr. Williams please come to emergency!"

A young man had arrived at emergency with a knife completely launched in his chest.

The call went out again. "Dr. Daniel Hale Williams come quickly to emergency?" "What is the problem? Where is the patient? Daniel asked.

This young man's life was at stake. His relatives had gathered in the lobby. Dr. Daniel could hear them praying and crying.

Daniel examined the young man. The knife was deep into his chest.

No surgeon had operated on the heart before. There was nothing written up for Daniel to make a decision from. Daniel explained to the young man's family.

"A doctor has never opened the thorax, the part of the body containing the heart and lungs. This is where the knife is launched. I must meet with my staff of doctors to decide the next step."

Dr. Daniel called his staff of doctors together. "We are at a dilemma," he said. "If we do not operate he will die. If we operate and he dies we will be criticized by other doctors.

Time is of the essence. We must make a quick decision.

What shall we do?" He asked. "Lets have a vote."

All the doctors said, "Yes, lets go for it. We took an oath to save lives."

Dr. Daniel Hale Williams went to the waiting room to speak to the family. "We must operate," he told the family. "If we do not operate now he will die. This operation will be the first of its kind. There is risk involved. We need your permission."

The mother said, "Dr. Williams you have our permission, we trust your judgement."

Dr. Daniel scrubbed up for surgery. With his students looking on, and his staff of doctors preparing to assist. Dr. Daniel prepared for the operation to remove the knife.

The nurse scrubbed and shaved the young mans chest with alcohol. The patient was now ready for surgery.

The patient was wheeled into the surgery room. There was a team of doctors waiting with Dr. Daniel Hale Williams.

Daniel pulled the sheet back from the patient's chest. He touched the chest lightly with his fingers where the knife was launched.

"Give me the saw." Said Dr. Daniel. He now explained. "I am now opening the thorax. I do not know what to expect."

Dr. Daniel stayed calm. A nurse wiped the sweat from his brow.

"This," he said, "is exploratory surgery. Make sure you document each step as I call it out." He said to his students. "No other surgeon has written papers on the subject, or documented such an operation. You must be precise in your recordings."

Dr. Daniel verbally talked his findings as he moved further into the chest to remove the knife.

"There is a small wound into the heart from the knife edge. There is also damage to the pericardium," he said.

"The wound to the heart we will not disturb. The wound to the pericardium we will repair."

"I am removing the knife." He gave the knife to the nurse.

"I am now sewing up the torn edges of the pericardium." He said. I am now sewing the chest back together.

"The patient is still alive. Clean the patient up. I want the patient watched until he is no longer in danger."

The operation was successful.

After the operation Daniel was so tired and he was mentally exhausted. He had successfully completed what no other doctor had dared to do.

He visited the family in the waiting room and told them the operation was a success. The knife was removed. The patient is now in the recovery room.

The family was pleased with this news.

Dr. Daniel Hale Williams returned to his office where some of the doctors were waiting for him.

"So this is what saving lives is all about," he said to his staff. "I am so pleased that the patient is still alive."

One of his staff doctors said, "Dr. Daniel Hale Williams, you are the best. You are not afraid to take chances. You worked so swiftly and with such ease and confidence."

Another doctor said to Daniel, "Dr. Daniel I have documented everything you said during the operation. I will have these notes typed. There is now a written guide for all doctors to follow."

All the doctors left to spread the word about the first successful open heart surgery by Dr. Daniel Hale Williams.

This medical breakthrough of open-heart surgery became good news for heart patients all over the world.

Daniel knew that Charles and his courage with scholar to detail changed the face of medicine forever.

"I have a urge to play a Game of Marbles," Daniel said to one of the assisting doctors as they prepared the patient for a blood transfusion. "Why a Game of Marbles Dr. Daniel Hale Williams." Daniel replied, "I attended the funeral of my best childhood friend, Dr. Charles Drew. Dr. Drew made it possible for us to save this patient's life with blood transfusions. He and I are still winning at marbles.

WOW!"